THE HOMEGROWN INVESTOR

PRIYANKA SRIVASTAVA

BLUEROSE PUBLISHERS
India | U.K.

Copyright © Priyanka Srivastava 2024

All rights reserved by author. No part of this publication may be reproduced, stored in a retrieval system or transmitted in any form or by any means, electronic, mechanical, photocopying, recording or otherwise, without the prior permission of the author. Although every precaution has been taken to verify the accuracy of the information contained herein, the publisher assume no responsibility for any errors or omissions. No liability is assumed for damages that may result from the use of information contained within.

BlueRose Publishers takes no responsibility for any damages, losses, or liabilities that may arise from the use or misuse of the information, products, or services provided in this publication.

For permissions requests or inquiries regarding this publication, please contact:

BLUEROSE PUBLISHERS
www.BlueRoseONE.com
info@bluerosepublishers.com
+91 8882 898 898
+4407342408967

ISBN: 978-93-6452-365-3

Cover design: Daksh
Typesetting: Tanya Raj Upadhyay

First Edition: November 2024

Introduction

The Homegrown Investor

By Priyanka Srivastava

The journey toward financial independence is as much about personal growth as it is about managing wealth. Through the years, I have had the privilege of meeting and learning from a diverse group of individuals who each embarked on their own unique financial journeys. These individuals, despite their varying backgrounds, experiences, and challenges, have one thing in common: they believed in the power of taking control of their financial destinies.

The Homegrown Investor is more than just a book about money. It is a tribute to all those who have shared their stories of resilience, courage, and thoughtful decision-making. Their experiences form the backbone of this book, offering not only practical insights but also deep inspiration for anyone looking to start or refine their own financial journey.

I want to express my deepest gratitude to each and every one of these participants. They have generously opened up their lives to share their successes, their mistakes, and the lessons they've learned along the way. These stories are not just about accumulating wealth—they are about creating a foundation of security, empowerment, and independence for oneself and one's family.

Through their journeys, we see the incredible impact of small, consistent steps toward financial health. Whether it was starting with a simple Systematic Investment Plan (SIP), buying a first property, or learning to diversify investments across asset classes, each person featured in this book has demonstrated that financial success is within reach for everyone.

This book is dedicated to those who have shown that even in the face of uncertainty or setbacks, it is possible to achieve financial security with patience, discipline, and a willingness to learn. I am honored to have been entrusted with their stories, and I hope their experiences inspire you to take your own steps toward financial freedom.

To those who shared their personal journeys with me: Thank you for your openness, your insights, and your courage. Your stories have enriched this book and will no doubt inspire many more to embrace the mindset of a *Homegrown Investor*.

With heartfelt thanks,
Priyanka Srivastava

The Remarkable Journey of Nirmala Tiwari: From Simple Savings to Strategic Investing

Nirmala Tiwari's story is one of quiet determination, financial wisdom, and an unwavering sense of responsibility towards her family, despite growing up in a time and place where women had little to no say in financial matters. Her journey is not just an account of how she managed to save and invest, but also a testament to how intention, discipline, and smart thinking can often outweigh formal education in shaping a successful financial future. Born in 1957 in Chokra, a small town in Barcholi, Jaunpur, Uttar Pradesh, India, Nirmala's life provides important lessons for modern women, particularly in the areas of saving, budgeting, and investing.

Early Life and Marriage in a Conservative Indian Family

Nirmala was born into a typical middle-class family. Her father, Ram Karan Tiwari, was a successful businessman who owned a flour mill. The family was part of a large joint household, comprising 50 members, all living together in a traditional setup. As with most families during that period, the household operated under a strict patriarchal system, where the male head of the family made most decisions. Women had limited autonomy, and their primary roles were restricted to household duties and raising children.

Nirmala's educational opportunities were similarly restricted. She was able to attend school only until class 5, which was not uncommon for girls in small towns during that time. Her father, like many men of his generation, did not prioritize his daughters' education and arranged Nirmala's marriage at a young age. She had no say in the matter, which reflected the social norms of the time. She accepted her fate without protest, as was expected of daughters in traditional Indian families.

Her husband, too, was still completing his education when they got married, and like Nirmala, came from a modest background. In 1979, he secured his first job with a salary of just Rs. 1,000 per month, a small sum even for that time, especially for a young couple with two children to support.

Financial Discipline in the Face of Scarcity

Despite having very little formal education, Nirmala demonstrated a natural understanding of financial discipline from the start. Managing a household with such a small income required immense resourcefulness and careful budgeting. While her husband's inclination was not towards saving, Nirmala took it upon herself to ensure that the family's future was financially secure. This was not easy given the limited resources, but she had a keen awareness of the importance of saving, even if it was just a small amount.

By 1981, Nirmala's husband was posted to the electricity department, and his salary increased to Rs. 1,400. By this time, the couple had four children. With growing expenses and a family to support, many people might have abandoned the idea of saving altogether, but Nirmala saw things differently. Instead of being discouraged by the added financial pressures, she focused on making the most out of what little money was left after household expenses.

Nirmala started small, with a recurring deposit (RD) of Rs. 100. While this may seem insignificant, it was a huge step for her given the family's limited financial resources. As time went on, and her confidence in her ability to manage money grew, she increased the RD to Rs. 200 and eventually Rs. 500.

Her strategy was simple yet effective: when each RD matured, she would reinvest the amount into a Fixed Deposit (FD). At that time, FDs offered good interest rates, unlike today's lower returns, and this allowed her savings to grow steadily over the years. What made this approach remarkable was not just Nirmala's persistence but also her ability to make long-term financial decisions without any formal training or education in finance. Her husband, who was largely disinterested in financial planning, wasn't even aware of how much she had saved. This quiet, unnoticed saving strategy became the foundation of the family's financial security in the years to come.

A Bold Financial Decision: Selling the VCR and TV

One particular incident highlights Nirmala's financial foresight and boldness in taking control of the family's finances. In the 1980s, her husband traveled abroad for work. During this trip, he bought a VCR, a highly coveted item at the time, and later purchased a color television locally. Owning such items in the 1980s was considered a status symbol, and her husband was understandably proud of these acquisitions.

However, Nirmala had a different perspective. She knew that while the VCR and television were luxurious purchases, they were not essential for the family's well-being. Without consulting her husband, she sold both the VCR and the TV for Rs. 16,000. With this money, she bought a smaller, more practical TV for the household and invested the remaining Rs. 12,000 in an FD. Her decision paid off handsomely. By 1993, the FD had grown to Rs. 100,000, a sum that proved to be invaluable when it came time to arrange her daughter's marriage.

This incident is a shining example of Nirmala's financial prudence. Despite societal norms that typically placed financial decision-making in the hands of men, Nirmala took control of the situation. Her ability to look beyond immediate gratification and focus on long-term financial stability proved to be a defining moment in her family's journey.

Transition from Saving to Investing

Nirmala's financial journey didn't end with saving. As she became more confident in her ability to manage money, she realized that merely saving wasn't enough. She needed to make her money work for her, which meant venturing into investing. This realization was a turning point in her financial evolution.

It was around this time that she came into contact with me, when I was working as a Branch Manager at a private bank. Recognizing her natural talent for managing money, I introduced her to the concept of investing. I explained how investing, as opposed to merely saving, could offer her higher returns over time and help grow her wealth more effectively.

Nirmala was quick to grasp these concepts, despite her limited formal education. She understood the importance of diversifying her investments and making sure her money wasn't just sitting in FDs but growing at a faster rate. She began by investing small amounts from her FDs and also allocated a portion of her husband's pension to monthly investments. This marked the beginning of a new chapter in Nirmala's financial journey—one that was driven by the power of compounding and strategic investing.

The Results of Disciplined Investing

Within just four years of disciplined investing, Nirmala saw her investments grow by more than 25%. This was no small feat, especially considering that she had started from scratch, with no formal education or financial background. Her ability to combine the traditional wisdom of saving with the modern strategy of investing set her apart from many of her contemporaries.

What makes Nirmala's story even more remarkable is the contrast between her approach and that of many younger women today. As a Branch Manager, I often observed that younger women, despite having more financial resources and education, tended to spend their husbands' earnings on non-essential luxuries like parties, shopping, and vacations. While enjoying life is important, many of these women failed to recognize the importance of saving and investing for the future.

In stark contrast, Nirmala, with her limited education and modest background, had the foresight to not only save but also grow her wealth. Her story serves as a powerful reminder that financial success is not determined by how much money one starts with, but by how wisely one manages it.

Lessons from Nirmala's Journey

Nirmala's journey offers several important lessons for women of all backgrounds, particularly those who may feel that they are at a disadvantage due to a lack of formal education or financial training.

1. **The Power of Intentional Saving:** Nirmala's ability to save, even in small amounts, was the cornerstone of her financial success. Her discipline in setting aside money regularly, no matter how little, is a lesson in the power of intentional saving. For women who may feel that they can't save because they don't earn much, Nirmala's story shows that every little bit counts.

2. **Long-Term Thinking:** Nirmala's decision to sell the VCR and TV and invest the proceeds into a long-term FD demonstrates the importance of thinking beyond immediate gratification. By focusing on the bigger picture, she was able to secure her family's future and finance important life events, like her daughter's wedding.

3. **Investing for Growth:** While saving is important, Nirmala understood that investing is what truly grows wealth over time. Her transition from saving to investing is a critical lesson for women who may be saving but not yet investing. By putting her money into higher-return instruments, Nirmala was able to multiply her savings and build a stronger financial foundation.

4. **Education is Not the Only Path to Financial Wisdom:** Nirmala's story shows that formal education is not a prerequisite for financial success. What matters most is the intention to save, the discipline to stick to a plan, and the willingness to learn about new opportunities like investing.

5. **Financial Independence:** Despite living in a traditional, patriarchal society, Nirmala took control of her family's financial future. Her journey is a powerful example of how women, even in restrictive environments, can take charge of their finances and make a lasting impact on their families.

Conclusion

Nirmala Tiwari's story is an inspiring example of how financial wisdom, discipline, and foresight can lead to success, regardless of one's educational background or societal constraints. Her ability to save, invest, and grow her family's wealth over time is a testament to the power of intentional financial planning.

From Housewife to Real Estate Queen: The Inspiring Journey of Tanima Shukla

Tanima Shukla's journey from a housewife to a real estate queen is a compelling story of resilience, foresight, and determination. Born in 1962 into a middle-class family, Tanima faced numerous challenges from a young age. Despite the odds, she managed to transform her life, ultimately building a successful real estate empire that spanned multiple cities and diversified into mutual fund investments. This is the remarkable story of how she went from being a struggling daughter of a railway worker to a financial powerhouse.

Early Life and Struggles

Tanima Shukla's father, Brij Kishore, was a dedicated railway worker. He was the breadwinner of the family, but tragedy struck when he died in a railway accident when Tanima was just five years old. As the youngest of three siblings and the only girl, Tanima witnessed her family crumble under the weight of financial and emotional difficulties following her father's untimely death.

The family's situation worsened with time. Tanima's mother, a widow in a conservative society, struggled not only to make ends meet but also to handle the societal pressures of being a single parent. The social stigma attached to widowhood in the 1960s compounded their troubles, as support from extended family and friends was minimal. Tanima's brothers, though older, showed little interest in supporting their mother or Tanima herself. They were detached and made little effort to alleviate the family's financial strain.

Tanima, however, was different. From a young age, she showed great promise in her studies. Despite her family's struggles, she was determined to pursue her education and find a way to help her mother. She was exceptionally bright and dedicated to her academics, which became her escape from the hardships at home. She realized that education would be her key to changing her life circumstances and worked tirelessly to excel in her studies.

Taking the First Steps Toward Financial Independence

Tanima's first taste of financial independence came when she began tutoring girls in her neighborhood. Initially, she offered free lessons, but as word spread and the number of students increased, she began charging Rs. 100 per student. This money, though small, was a lifeline for her family. It helped ease some of the financial burdens her mother faced and gave Tanima a sense of pride and accomplishment. More importantly, it gave her early exposure to the concept of earning and saving money.

While her brothers continued to distance themselves from the family's financial troubles, Tanima stepped up to the plate. She completed her education and went on to pursue a post-graduation in Economics. In 1985, she completed her master's degree, giving her a solid understanding of money management, economic theories, and financial planning. However, she still lacked the resources to implement the skills she had acquired through her studies.

Marriage and the Awakening of Her Financial Instincts

In the same year she completed her post-graduation, Tanima got married to Rajesh Shukla, a merchant mariner by profession. Rajesh came from a financially stable family, but despite his decent income, he was not much of a saver. When Tanima married Rajesh, she was surprised to find that despite working for over a decade, he had only Rs. 300 in his bank account. This was a shocking realization for Tanima. Her inner economist was shaken to the core when she realized that her husband, who had been earning a substantial salary for years, had no significant savings or investments to show for it.

Tanima's immediate concern was the lack of financial security in Rajesh's job. As a merchant mariner, Rajesh had no pension or long-term financial safety net. His job was high-paying but unstable, and without a structured savings plan, the couple faced an uncertain future. This realization marked the beginning of Tanima's active involvement in managing the family's finances. She knew she had to take charge to ensure their financial security and began looking for ways to save and invest their limited funds.

The First Investment: Kisan Vikas Patra (KVP)

In 1985, shortly after her marriage, Tanima received Rs. 500 as a gift from her family. She immediately went to the post office and purchased Kisan Vikas Patra (KVP), a government savings scheme that offered attractive interest rates at the time. For Tanima, this was a moment of great pride and joy—her first real investment. Though small, it marked the beginning of her journey towards financial independence. Her husband, Rajesh, was supportive but remained mostly uninvolved in the management of their finances, trusting Tanima to take care of their savings and investments.

Rajesh's salary at the time was Rs. 5,000 per month, and Tanima's mother-in-law gave her Rs. 300 each month for household expenses. Despite the limited budget, Tanima found ways to save whatever little she could. Over time, she managed to build a modest amount of savings, which she would later use for larger investments.

The First Real Estate Investment

In 1988, Rajesh switched jobs and joined a bigger company, where he was soon promoted. This brought some financial relief and allowed Tanima to focus on expanding their savings. Tanima knew that saving alone would not be enough to secure their future, and her background in economics had taught her the importance of investing in assets that would appreciate over time. Real estate caught her attention as an investment avenue.

With some money saved and a loan of Rs. 25,000 from her mother, Tanima convinced Rajesh to invest in property. Rajesh was initially hesitant, unsure of the risks involved, but Tanima was determined. She used her knowledge of economics and market trends to persuade him, and they bought their first property in Delhi. Unfortunately, this initial investment did not turn out as well as Tanima had hoped. The property's value did not appreciate as expected, and after several years, they were forced to sell it at a loss.

While the experience was discouraging, Tanima did not let it deter her. She understood that real estate was a long-term game and that losses were part of the learning process. In 1991, she reinvested the money from the sale of the first property into a new property. This time, she was more strategic in her approach, selecting a location with better growth potential.

At the same time, Tanima continued to invest in small savings schemes like KVP and recurring deposits (RDs) at the bank. The interest rates on these savings instruments were relatively high during that period, which gave her good returns on her small investments. These additional savings helped her stay afloat during the ups and downs of her real estate ventures.

Building a Real Estate Portfolio

By the early 1990s, Tanima's persistence in real estate began to pay off. The second property they purchased started appreciating in value, and they put it up for rent, which gave them a steady stream of income. This was a turning point in Tanima's financial journey. With the rental income providing some financial stability, Tanima began to focus more aggressively on building their real estate portfolio.

In the following years, Tanima and Rajesh purchased two more properties—one for their own residence and another for rental purposes—in Lucknow. These properties proved to be excellent investments, as the real estate market in Lucknow experienced significant growth during that time.

In 1998, Tanima made one of her most successful real estate investments when she bought a commercial property in Greater Kailash, New Delhi, for Rs. 12 lakhs. This property turned out to be a goldmine. Within just three years, its value skyrocketed, and they sold it for Rs. 48 lakhs, earning a massive profit. This sale marked the moment when Tanima's real estate empire truly began to take shape.

Tanima's sharp financial instincts and ability to spot opportunities had transformed her from a housewife managing small savings into a savvy investor with a growing portfolio of properties. By the time she was 39, she and Rajesh had acquired 11 properties, some of which were still generating rental income while others had been sold for a profit.

The Shift to Mutual Funds: Diversifying the Investment Portfolio

By the early 2000s, Tanima had built a substantial real estate portfolio, but she was not content to stop there. She understood that real estate, while lucrative, had its risks, and she wanted to diversify their investments to ensure long-term financial security.

With the money they had earned from their real estate ventures, Tanima began exploring the world of mutual funds. She had learned about the benefits of diversification during her post-graduation studies in economics, and she knew that mutual funds could provide a balanced investment option with less risk compared to real estate. She started investing systematically in mutual funds, using the profits from their real estate sales to build a diversified portfolio.

Tanima's foray into mutual funds was yet another success. Over the years, her investments in equity and debt funds grew steadily, complementing the rental income from their real estate holdings. The combination of real estate and mutual fund investments provided Tanima and Rajesh with a diversified, well-rounded financial portfolio that gave them both security and financial freedom.

Lessons Learned: Key Takeaways from Tanima's Journey

1. **Education and Financial Literacy:** Tanima's post-graduation in economics played a crucial role in shaping her financial mindset. Her knowledge of money management, investment, and economics gave her the foundation to make informed decisions. This highlights the importance of financial literacy in achieving long-term financial success.

2. **Perseverance and Learning from Failure:** Tanima's first real estate investment did not go as planned, but instead of giving up, she learned from her mistakes and reinvested strategically. Her journey underscores the importance of perseverance and learning from setbacks.

3. **Diversification is Key:** While real estate was her primary investment vehicle, Tanima understood the importance of diversification. Her decision to invest in mutual funds helped balance the risks associated with real estate and provided her with a more stable financial foundation.

4. **Taking Control of Finances:** Tanima's decision to take charge of her family's finances was a turning point in her

life. She recognized that without a proper financial plan, they would never achieve financial security. Her story is a reminder that taking control of one's finances is essential for long-term success.

5. **Long-Term Vision:** Tanima's success was not an overnight achievement. It took years of careful planning, saving, and investing to build her real estate empire. Her story highlights the importance of having a long-term vision and being patient with investments.

Conclusion: From Housewife to Financial Powerhouse

Tanima Shukla's journey from a middle-class housewife to a real estate queen is a story of courage, determination, and financial acumen. Despite the early challenges she faced in life, she used her education and financial instincts to build a successful real estate empire that provided her family with financial security. Today, Tanima's portfolio includes both real estate and mutual fund investments, making her a true example of financial empowerment.

Her story is an inspiration to women everywhere, proving that with the right knowledge, mindset, and perseverance, it is possible to achieve financial independence and success. From managing small savings in a post office scheme to owning multiple properties across India, Tanima's journey is a testament to the power of smart investing and the transformative impact it can have on one's life.

The Remarkable Financial Journey of Shalu Bansal: From Childhood Savings to Financial Mastery

Shalu Bansal's story is one of vision, discipline, and financial acumen. Born in 1977 into a well-to-do business class family, Shalu's upbringing was markedly different from that of many children in similar economic environments. While many children from affluent families grow up with little regard for the value of money, Shalu's father instilled in her a habit of saving from an early age. This early financial education laid the foundation for a life characterized by smart investments, strategic planning, and financial independence.

Shalu's journey from a child saving her pocket money to an adult who expertly navigated the complexities of mutual funds, real estate, and other financial instruments is both inspiring and instructive. Through her life, she demonstrated that financial success is not just a product of earning more but of making informed decisions and growing wealth steadily over time.

Early Life and the Seeds of Financial Responsibility

Shalu Bansal was born into a family that was financially secure, with her father running a successful business. Despite the family's affluence, her father was deeply committed to teaching his children about the importance of financial responsibility. From the age of nine, Shalu began receiving pocket money, a modest sum of Rs. 50 per month—a considerable amount for a child at that time. With limited options to spend her money, Shalu initially enjoyed spending her pocket money on food and clothes. However, her father's lessons in saving had already begun to take root. Even at such a young age, she was mindful of putting aside at least Rs. 25 each month.

By the time Shalu was 12, her father rewarded her responsible attitude by gifting her a two-wheeler for convenience. The vehicle, costing Rs. 11,000, wasn't a fully parental gift, though—Shalu contributed Rs. 3,000 from her savings, with her father covering the remaining Rs. 8,000. At an age when most children focus on spending, Shalu was already shouldering financial responsibilities. This early experience not only reinforced her understanding of the value of money but also helped her realize the importance of saving for future goals.

Educational Pursuits and Inclination Towards Finance

Shalu's academic path naturally aligned with her growing interest in finance. She went on to pursue an MBA from Jaipuriya College in Lucknow, Uttar Pradesh, where she further honed her financial skills. Her studies provided her with the theoretical understanding of finance and economics, which she later applied practically in her life. Her academic journey equipped her with the knowledge and confidence to make informed financial decisions and set her up for a life focused on managing and growing wealth.

Marriage and the Beginning of Her Financial Journey

In 2002, Shalu married Pawan, a government officer. While Pawan came from a stable background, he wasn't particularly focused on saving money. Like many people, Pawan had not accumulated any significant savings at the time of their marriage. This, however, did not discourage Shalu. Instead, she took it upon herself to manage their finances and instill better saving habits into their married life.

Shalu quickly assumed the role of financial planner for the family. With her eye always on the future, she began saving whatever portion of Pawan's salary she could manage. By 2003, Shalu had saved Rs. 90,000, and together with Pawan's support, she made her first major investment: a property worth Rs. 3,40,000. To finance this purchase, she took out a loan of Rs. 2,40,000 from the bank, but her Rs. 90,000 contribution was entirely from her personal savings. It was a significant milestone in her financial journey and an early indication of her ability to make smart, calculated decisions.

Systematic Investment Plans and Debt Management

Even while managing the housing loan, Shalu began exploring other financial instruments to strengthen her portfolio. In 2003, she initiated her first Systematic Investment Plan (SIP) with Rs. 500 in well-known mutual funds, including HDFC, Franklin Templeton, and Reliance. Her goal was to allow these small, consistent investments to grow over time, providing her with the financial leverage needed to manage larger goals.

Over the next five years, Shalu's SIPs performed remarkably well, yielding an impressive return of 22%. She used this return to reduce her housing loan, a strategic move that showcased her understanding of how to balance debt with long-term investments. By consistently making small contributions to her SIPs and allowing the power of compounding to work its magic, Shalu was able to manage her debt and grow her wealth at the same time.

Expanding Investments: Real Estate and Mutual Funds

Shalu's financial journey didn't stop with her first property purchase. By 2005, she had recognized the importance of diversifying her investments. She started another SIP, this time in the name of her mother, with an initial investment of Rs. 500. Over the years, she steadily increased this SIP, and by 2023, it had grown to an impressive Rs. 80,000. Her commitment to consistent, long-term investing was yielding substantial rewards, and her mother's portfolio was a testament to Shalu's financial foresight.

Shalu didn't just limit herself to SIPs. She also took proactive steps to ensure her children's education and future financial stability. In 2016 and 2017, she sought financial consultancy from Tata, taking expert advice to plan her children's education and marriage. In addition to her SIPs, she began making lump-sum investments in mutual funds, strategically timing these investments to align with her long-term goals.

Shalu's portfolio was further diversified through non-convertible debentures (NCDs). In 2010, she began investing in NCDs at an interest rate of 9.50%, ensuring that she had regular cash inflows when the debentures matured every three years. Each time an NCD matured, Shalu reinvested the funds into mutual funds, creating a cycle of continuous growth for her wealth. By constantly reinvesting her returns, she was able to maximize her gains without taking on excessive risk.

Real Estate Success: Strategic Purchases and Sales

While mutual funds and SIPs formed the backbone of Shalu's financial strategy, real estate remained an essential part of her portfolio. In 2010, Shalu made one of her most significant investments by purchasing a plot for Rs. 14 lakhs. She had a long-term vision for the property, knowing that real estate could offer considerable appreciation over time.

Her patience paid off when, in 2021, she sold the property for an astounding Rs. 1 crore. This investment had grown more than sevenfold in just over a decade. True to her disciplined approach, Shalu didn't splurge the proceeds from the sale. Instead, she reinvested half of the profits back into real estate and allocated the remaining half to mutual funds. This careful balance between real estate and mutual funds ensured that she continued to grow her wealth without overexposing herself to a single asset class.

Sovereign Gold Bonds: Another Layer of Security

Shalu's approach to investing was thorough and diverse. In addition to mutual funds, real estate, and NCDs, she also made regular investments in Sovereign Gold Bonds. These bonds, backed by the Government of India, offered Shalu the dual benefit of capital appreciation and interest earnings. Each year, she increased her investments in these bonds, providing her with a secure and stable form of wealth accumulation that complemented her more aggressive investments in mutual funds and real estate.

Shalu's portfolio by this point had evolved into a well-diversified mix of assets that provided her with a steady income stream, capital growth, and long-term financial security. Her commitment to regularly reviewing and adjusting her investments meant that she was always prepared for market fluctuations, ensuring that her wealth continued to grow.

The Power of Financial Discipline

What sets Shalu Bansal apart is not just her financial success but the discipline and foresight that got her there. From her early days of saving pocket money to her sophisticated portfolio of real estate, mutual funds, NCDs, and gold bonds, Shalu's journey is a testament to the power of consistent, long-term financial planning.

Her story is a powerful example of how the principles of saving and investing can transform not just personal wealth but an entire family's financial future. Shalu's ability to manage her family's finances, reduce debt, and grow her investments reflects the importance of financial literacy, discipline, and a willingness to explore various investment options.

Conclusion

Shalu Bansal's financial journey is an inspiring example of what can be achieved with discipline, education, and a strategic approach to saving and investing. From the early lessons imparted by her father to her impressive portfolio of mutual funds, real estate, and gold bonds, Shalu's life is a blueprint for financial success. Her ability to balance her family's needs, make smart investments, and continually grow her wealth over time serves as a model for anyone looking to achieve long-term financial independence.

Shalu's story is a reminder that financial success is not just about earning more but about making your money work for you. By starting early, staying disciplined, and diversifying her investments, Shalu transformed herself from a young girl with Rs. 50 in pocket money into a financially savvy woman with a substantial portfolio of assets. Her journey is proof that with the right mindset, anyone can achieve financial freedom.

The Financial Transformation of Priyanka Tondon: A Story of Saving, Learning, and Growth

Priyanka Tondon's story is a testament to the power of financial awareness, discipline, and guidance. Born into a middle-class family, Priyanka was taught the importance of saving from a young age, thanks to her father, who worked in a bank. This early education laid the foundation for her future financial decisions, though her journey wasn't always smooth. Like many people, Priyanka faced financial challenges, but with determination, careful planning, and timely advice, she and her husband, Abhishek, turned their financial situation around.

Priyanka's journey offers valuable lessons on how a woman, even as a housewife, can play a crucial role in wealth-building for her family.

Early Life and the Habit of Saving

Priyanka was born into a middle-class family where financial prudence was a core value. Her father, who worked in a bank, was instrumental in teaching her the importance of saving. She grew up in a modest household, where every rupee was valued, and the habit of setting aside money was ingrained from childhood. This early exposure to the importance of saving would later influence her approach to financial planning.

During her school and college years, Priyanka was like any other young girl, enjoying life, but always aware of the need to save money. She often set aside a portion of her pocket money and whatever small earnings she could generate from part-time work. Her father's job in the bank also meant she was exposed to basic concepts of finance, such as fixed deposits and recurring deposits, though she had yet to delve deeply into the world of investments.

Early Career and First Exposure to the Stock Market

After completing her graduation, Priyanka didn't immediately step into a serious career. Instead, she took up a temporary position with Kotak Securities, followed by a stint at UTI Securities. This was more out of curiosity and the desire to explore the corporate world than a planned career move. However, it was during these short-term jobs that Priyanka was introduced to the stock market, an area that piqued her interest.

Despite her growing curiosity about stocks and investments, Priyanka's income from these jobs was relatively modest. She wasn't earning enough to make significant investments, and her lifestyle didn't demand much either. This period was more about learning than building wealth. Her exposure to stocks and the financial markets, though brief, left a lasting impression on her, and she realized the potential of investing in wealth creation.

Marriage and Financial Concerns

In 2008, Priyanka's life took a new turn when she married Abhishek Tondon, a Merchant Mariner. Abhishek had been working in his field since 2000, and while his job paid well, Priyanka was surprised to learn that Abhishek hadn't managed to save much. Apart from a few investments in gold, there wasn't much financial security or planning in place.

This realization worried Priyanka. She had always been mindful of saving, but now, as a wife and soon-to-be mother, she became acutely aware of the need for financial security. With Abhishek's job requiring him to be away for extended periods, Priyanka took on the responsibility of managing the household finances. However, she felt overwhelmed by the task. Their income was substantial, but without a clear savings plan or investment strategy, she feared they wouldn't be able to build the kind of future they wanted for themselves and their children.

In 2010, Priyanka gave birth to their first child, and the need for financial planning became even more pressing. To ensure some security, she decided to take out life insurance. However, over time, this decision proved less effective than she had hoped. The life insurance plan didn't provide the returns or peace of mind she was looking for, leaving her still searching for a better solution.

The Turning Point: Meeting a Financial Advisor

The major turning point in Priyanka and Abhishek's financial journey came in 2017 when Priyanka met Mohd Ahmar Farooqui, a banker from YES BANK. Up until this point, the couple had made one significant financial decision—they had purchased a property in 2012. However, this purchase left them financially stretched, as much of their income was going towards interest payments on the loan. As a result, they had little left to save or invest, and their financial growth was stagnant.

Ahmar's entry into their lives was nothing short of transformative. He sat down with Priyanka and Abhishek and helped them understand the importance of systematic investments. He introduced them to the concept of Systematic Investment Plans (SIPs), which would allow them to invest small, manageable amounts regularly into mutual funds. SIPs would not only help them build wealth over time but also reduce the financial strain they were feeling from their loan payments.

Ahmar's advice to Priyanka was clear: Start small but be consistent, and increase the SIP contributions each year. Following his advice, Priyanka and Abhishek began their SIP journey, starting with a modest amount. They were careful to stick to the plan, and over time, as their income allowed, they increased their SIP contributions.

Early Payoff: Reducing the Housing Loan

One of the immediate benefits of starting the SIPs was the discipline it instilled in their financial habits. As the SIPs began to grow, Priyanka found herself in a stronger financial position. The regular returns from the SIPs, coupled with the power of compounding, gave them a financial cushion they hadn't experienced before.

Within a few years, Priyanka and Abhishek had accumulated enough wealth through their SIPs to make an early repayment on their housing loan. This was a huge relief for the couple, as it freed them from the burden of high-interest payments and allowed them to focus on other financial goals.

Building a Portfolio: Second Property and Beyond

With the housing loan repaid, Priyanka and Abhishek were in a much stronger financial position. Priyanka, ever mindful of the importance of diversifying their assets, decided to invest in another property. They purchased their second property, marking another milestone in their financial journey. This time, they were more financially secure and didn't face the same pressures as with their first property purchase.

By now, Priyanka had fully embraced her role as the family's financial planner. Though she was a housewife, she understood that wealth building wasn't solely a man's responsibility. Priyanka made it a point to educate herself continuously about various investment options, and she was keenly aware of the importance of long-term planning.

Expanding Beyond SIPs: A Growing Portfolio

Priyanka's success with SIPs didn't stop her from exploring other investment opportunities. As their financial situation improved, she began to diversify their portfolio even further. She and Abhishek continued to increase their SIP contributions each year, but they also began exploring other forms of investments, such as equities, debt funds, and fixed deposits.

Priyanka had learned a valuable lesson from her early foray into life insurance: Not all financial products are created equal, and it's crucial to understand the long-term returns and risks associated with each investment. With the guidance of Ahmar, she ensured that every investment they made was aligned with their financial goals, whether it was saving for their children's education or planning for their retirement.

Financial Empowerment and a Bright Future

Priyanka's story is one of financial empowerment. Despite being a housewife, she played an active role in managing her family's wealth and ensuring a secure future for her children. Her journey from someone who was initially unsure about managing finances to a confident, informed investor is inspiring.

Today, Priyanka and Abhishek enjoy a well-rounded financial portfolio. Their SIPs continue to grow, providing them with regular returns and peace of mind. Their property investments have also appreciated, adding to their wealth. Priyanka's financial decisions, particularly the early repayment of their housing loan and the disciplined approach to SIPs, have given the family financial freedom and security.

One of the key takeaways from Priyanka's journey is the importance of seeking professional advice. Meeting Ahmar was a turning point, but it was Priyanka's willingness to take his advice and implement a long-term strategy that made all the difference. Her story also highlights the importance of consistency—whether it's in saving, investing, or paying off debt. Small, regular contributions, when done consistently over time, can lead to significant financial growth.

Conclusion

Priyanka Tondon's financial journey is a reminder that wealth-building is not reserved for those with high-paying jobs or significant financial expertise. Through discipline, a willingness to learn, and the right guidance, anyone can take control of their financial future. Priyanka's story is particularly inspiring for women, showing that even as a housewife, one can play a pivotal role in managing and growing a family's wealth.

Today, Priyanka and Abhishek are reaping the rewards of their disciplined financial planning. Their journey is a testament to the power of small, consistent steps, and their story serves as an example for anyone looking to build wealth and achieve financial freedom.

The Transformational Journey of Ritu Singh: From Cluelessness to Financial Mastery

Ritu Singh's life is a story of transformation—of a woman who, despite being labeled unintelligent and facing immense challenges, rose to build a strong financial portfolio and achieve financial independence. Born into a middle-class family, Ritu was never considered a bright student, and her life seemed directionless for many years. However, through sheer determination and a desire to create a better future for herself and her child, Ritu transformed her life, eventually becoming a financially successful and independent woman.

This 4,000-word account chronicles her struggles, her rise from a small salary to creating a significant financial portfolio, and how she became a role model for women who seek financial independence and empowerment.

Early Life and Academic Struggles

Ritu Singh was born into a modest middle-class family. From an early age, it was apparent to her family that Ritu was different from her siblings, who excelled in academics and were considered smart. Ritu, on the other hand, struggled to keep up with her studies. She wasn't a naturally gifted student and often found herself labeled as "dumb" in comparison to her siblings. This label, which followed her throughout her childhood, affected her confidence. She frequently felt lost, and her lack of academic success became a constant source of worry for her parents.

While her siblings were praised for their academic achievements, Ritu found herself receiving little guidance or support in finding her strengths. This lack of direction left her feeling confused about her future, as she had no clear vision of what she wanted to do with her life. She barely managed to pass her school exams, and her graduation was no different. After completing her degree, she was still directionless, unsure of what career to pursue, and with no one to guide her.

Early Marriage and Financial Struggles

With no clear plan for her future, Ritu's parents, concerned about her prospects, arranged her marriage at a young age. She married Sanjay, a man who, at first, seemed capable of providing for her. But soon after their marriage, it became clear that Ritu's lack of financial independence was going to be a major challenge. Sanjay, while earning a decent income, was not generous with household finances. He saved the majority of his earnings and provided Ritu with very little for the running of the household.

Ritu found herself in a difficult position. She had no savings of her own, no financial knowledge, and was entirely dependent on Sanjay for money. To make matters worse, she had never cultivated the habit of saving, even as a child. When she had received pocket money, she spent it freely without thinking of the future. Now, as a married woman and soon a mother, she began to realize just how important it was to have her own source of income.

In the first few years of her marriage, Ritu gave birth to her first child. The financial pressure mounted, as Sanjay continued to provide only minimal financial support, leaving Ritu to manage the household on a shoestring budget. Frustrated with her lack of financial control and her growing dependence on Sanjay, Ritu began to feel the desire to stand on her own feet. She didn't want to rely on someone else to provide for her or her child, and she began to dream of becoming financially independent.

Separation and the Decision to Stand on Her Own

After five years of marriage, Ritu reached her breaking point. The financial strain, combined with Sanjay's lack of support, had become unbearable. They decided to part ways. The separation left Ritu alone to care for her child, with no financial backup or safety net. It was a tough decision, but Ritu knew that she had to take control of her life. She could no longer afford to be dependent on someone else for her livelihood.

In the wake of her separation, Ritu faced a harsh reality: she had no income and no job experience. But she was determined to make a change. She knew she needed to earn money not only to support herself but also to provide for her child. After the separation, she found her first small job. It didn't pay much—only Rs. 6,000 per month—but it was enough to cover the bare essentials. More importantly, it was the first step toward her financial independence.

While the job provided some financial relief, it wasn't enough to create long-term stability. The salary was too low to support both herself and her child in the way she wanted. After a few months, Ritu realized that she needed a better job with a higher salary if she was to secure a future for herself and her child. With a renewed sense of determination, she began applying for other positions, hoping to find something that would allow her to grow professionally and financially.

A New Beginning: Corporate Life and Financial Education

Ritu's perseverance paid off when she was offered a job in a corporate office. This new role offered her a significantly higher salary, and while she was initially intimidated by the corporate environment, Ritu embraced the challenge. She worked hard, learning everything she could about her job and the corporate world. With each passing month, she became more confident in her abilities.

As her salary grew, Ritu became more aware of the importance of financial planning. She began reading books and articles on personal finance, determined to educate herself about money management. It was during this period that she came across the concept of systematic investment plans (SIPs). She realized that in order to secure her financial future, she needed to start investing.

When Ritu's salary reached Rs. 10,000 per month, she started her first SIP with a modest Rs. 2,000 investment. It was a small amount, but it was the beginning of her journey toward wealth creation. She was determined to make her money work for her, and SIPs offered her a way to grow her savings steadily over time.

Growing Wealth Through SIPs

Ritu's decision to invest in SIPs marked a turning point in her financial journey. As her salary increased, she gradually increased the amount of her SIP contributions. She was disciplined in her approach, making sure to invest consistently every month. Over time, the power of compounding worked in her favor, and her investments began to grow.

Seven years into her corporate career, Ritu had saved enough to make her first major investment: she purchased her first property. This was a significant achievement for her, especially considering that just a few years earlier, she had been struggling to make ends meet. The property became a valuable asset, and Ritu was careful to manage it well.

Five years later, she sold the property for a substantial profit, and instead of spending the money, she reinvested the proceeds into mutual funds. By this point, Ritu had become a savvy investor. She had learned the importance of diversifying her investments and was careful not to put all her money into one asset class. Her mutual fund investments began to grow, and she continued to increase her SIP contributions as her salary rose.

Avoiding Traditional Investment Routes

Unlike many others, Ritu didn't follow the traditional route of investing in fixed deposits (FDs), public provident funds (PPF), or the National Pension System (NPS). While these are considered safe investment options, Ritu believed in the power of market-linked instruments like mutual funds. She had done her research and understood that while mutual funds carried more risk, they also had the potential for higher returns in the long run. Ritu was willing to take calculated risks, and her decision paid off.

By avoiding the conventional, low-return investments, Ritu was able to grow her portfolio much faster. She became more confident in her financial decisions and continued to invest aggressively in SIPs, equity mutual funds, and other market-linked instruments. Her goal was to create a substantial financial cushion that would provide her with long-term security and freedom.

Achieving Financial Independence

Through years of hard work, disciplined investing, and smart financial decisions, Ritu built a portfolio worth crores. She had come a long way from the young woman who had struggled academically and faced financial hardships in her marriage. Now, she was financially independent, with a portfolio that provided her with a steady stream of income.

Ritu's journey was not just about accumulating wealth—it was about reclaiming her life. She had proved to herself and others that financial success wasn't reserved for those with high-paying jobs or exceptional academic records. It was about discipline, determination, and the willingness to learn.

Lessons from Ritu Singh's Journey

Ritu Singh's life offers several valuable lessons, especially for women who aspire to achieve financial independence:

1. **It's Never Too Late to Start:** Ritu's financial journey didn't begin until after her separation from Sanjay. Despite her late start, she was able to build a substantial portfolio through consistent investing and smart financial decisions. Her story shows that it's never too late to take control of your financial future.

2. **Education is Key:** Even though Ritu wasn't academically gifted, she made the effort to educate herself about finance. She read books, followed financial news, and sought out resources to help her understand the best investment options. This education empowered her to make informed decisions and grow her wealth.

3. **Discipline and Consistency Matter:** Ritu's success was built on the foundation of disciplined saving and investing. She didn't waver in her commitment to investing, even when her salary was small. By consistently contributing to her SIPs, she was able to harness the power of compounding and build significant wealth over time.

4. **Diversification is Important:** Ritu didn't rely on just one type of investment. She diversified her portfolio across different asset classes, which helped her manage risk while maximizing returns. This strategy allowed her to grow her wealth steadily while minimizing the impact of market fluctuations.

5. **Take Calculated Risks:** Ritu's decision to invest in mutual funds rather than traditional options like FDs or PPFs was a calculated risk. While market-linked investments carry more risk, they also offer higher returns. Ritu's willingness to take these risks allowed her to grow her portfolio faster than if she had stuck to safer, lower-return investments.

6. **Financial Independence is Empowering:** Ritu's journey shows how empowering it can be for women to take control of their finances. Her financial independence gave her the freedom to make her own decisions, support her child, and live life on her own terms.

Conclusion

Ritu Singh's journey from a directionless, financially dependent woman to a financially independent success story is an inspiration to anyone who has ever doubted their ability to achieve financial security. Despite her struggles in school, her early marriage, and the financial hardships she faced, Ritu was able to turn her life around through education, discipline, and smart investing.

The Financial Journey of Shikha Sharma: From Pampered Child to Self-Made Woman

Shikha Sharma's life is a story of transformation, independence, and financial resilience. The youngest in her family, Shikha was pampered as a child, living in a comfortable household where her father's government job provided stability. She grew up in a secure environment, but her journey into adulthood and financial independence was marked by personal struggles, hard-earned lessons, and eventual success. Shikha's life offers valuable insights into the power of self-reliance, disciplined investing, and the importance of making informed financial choices.

This 4,000-word narrative explores Shikha's transformation from a carefree young girl to a financially savvy and independent woman, highlighting the challenges she overcame and the strategies she used to build her wealth.

Early Life: A Comfortable Yet Sheltered Childhood

Shikha Sharma was the youngest among her siblings and the most pampered child in her family. Her father worked a stable government job, which ensured that the family never faced financial difficulties. Shikha grew up in an environment where money wasn't a major concern, and as a result, she never gave much thought to saving or managing finances. Unlike many children from middle-class families who were taught the value of money early on, Shikha was sheltered from such responsibilities. Her needs were always met, and financial discipline was not a priority for her.

The family's financial security took a turn when Shikha's father passed away. This loss was compounded when her mother also passed away not long after. The burden of running the household fell squarely on the shoulders of Shikha's elder sister, who took it upon herself to manage the family's finances and look after her siblings. She was the authority in the family, and her decisions were respected by everyone, including Shikha.

Shikha's elder sister, out of a sense of duty and responsibility, decided not to marry and instead dedicated her life to the family. With her taking charge, Shikha had little reason to worry about money or plan for her future. She was a bright student and had aspirations of building a career after completing her education. However, her sister's influence and the pressure to follow traditional norms led Shikha to marry early, despite her own dreams of working and being financially independent.

Marriage: A New Set of Challenges

Shikha's marriage marked the beginning of a challenging period in her life. Although she had agreed to the marriage out of respect for her sister's wishes, she quickly realized that her new life was far from what she had imagined. Financially, things were not as stable as they had been in her parental home. Her husband wasn't supportive, and the marriage soon became a source of personal and financial strain.

Shikha found herself in a difficult situation. She had no savings, no financial plan, and was emotionally and financially dependent on her husband. Her personal life was far from happy, and after enduring a few years of an unfulfilling and difficult marriage, Shikha made the brave decision to separate from her husband. This decision, while liberating, also brought with it the harsh reality of having to fend for herself without any financial safety net.

The First Steps Toward Financial Independence

After her separation, Shikha was faced with the daunting task of building a life on her own. With no savings or job experience, she knew that the path ahead would not be easy. However, she was determined to regain control of her life, and the first step was finding a job. She secured a position at an insurance company, a modest beginning, but one that offered her the opportunity to earn her own income for the first time.

Shikha's salary was small, and managing her own expenses for the first time was a challenge. Yet, she understood the importance of saving and investing, even if the amounts were small. In 2000, she started her first systematic investment plan (SIP) with a modest Rs. 1,000 contribution. This was the first financial decision that would lay the foundation for her future success.

Every year, Shikha made it a point to increase her SIP contribution as her salary grew. She understood that inflation would erode the value of her savings if she didn't consistently increase her investments. By the end of five years, her SIP had grown to Rs. 5,000 per month. As she continued to work and gain experience in the insurance sector, her earnings grew, and she made sure to increase her SIP contributions accordingly.

The Importance of Diversification: From SIPs to Fixed Deposits

Shikha knew that simply saving wasn't enough; she had to make her money work for her. While SIPs were a good start, she also wanted to diversify her investments to ensure she was prepared for the future. Every five years, she converted a portion of her accumulated SIP funds into fixed deposits (FDs), ensuring that she had some risk-free investments to fall back on in case of emergencies.

Her strategy was simple but effective: keep increasing the SIP contributions while periodically converting a portion of the returns into FDs. This allowed her to balance the higher risk of market-linked investments with the safety of traditional, low-risk instruments like fixed deposits. By 2010, her SIP contributions had grown to Rs. 15,000 per month, and she had built a small but solid financial foundation.

Facing the Reality of Inflation and Taking Bigger Risks

As Shikha became more financially literate, she realized that even her steadily growing SIP contributions weren't enough to secure her long-term financial future. The cost of living was rising, and inflation was eroding the value of her savings faster than she had anticipated. She knew she needed to take more significant steps to build real wealth.

Around this time, Shikha began exploring real estate as an investment option. She knew that property could offer substantial returns over time, especially if bought and sold wisely. With her savings from SIPs and FDs, she started buying small properties. She wasn't a traditional investor who bought properties to hold for decades. Instead, Shikha adopted a more active approach. She purchased small properties, held onto them for a few years until their value appreciated, and then sold them for a profit.

The profits from these property sales were reinvested into mutual funds and SIPs, further diversifying her portfolio. Real estate became a crucial part of her investment strategy, offering her significant returns while also giving her the flexibility to liquidate assets when needed. Shikha was careful to keep her portfolio balanced between real estate, mutual funds, and safer investments like fixed deposits.

Building a Portfolio: The Power of Consistency

Shikha's approach to wealth-building was marked by consistency and discipline. Over the years, she continued to invest in SIPs, increase her contributions, and make smart decisions about her real estate investments. She wasn't afraid to take risks, but her risks were always calculated, and she made sure to do her research before making any major financial decisions.

By the time she was in her late 30s, Shikha had built a diversified and robust portfolio. She had investments in mutual funds, fixed deposits, and real estate, and her consistent SIP contributions were yielding substantial returns. She had also sold several properties, and the profits were reinvested wisely. Shikha was no longer the financially dependent woman she had been after her separation. She was now financially independent, with a growing portfolio that provided her with both security and opportunities for further growth.

The Challenges of Being a Single Woman Investor

Being a single woman in the world of finance and investments wasn't easy for Shikha. She didn't have a partner to guide or support her, and she often felt overwhelmed by the sheer complexity of the financial markets. She had to rely on her own judgment and the financial knowledge she gained over time. Shikha faced her fair share of challenges—whether it was navigating the complexities of real estate transactions or making sure her mutual fund investments were yielding the best returns.

Despite these challenges, Shikha remained focused on her goals. She sought advice from financial advisors when necessary, but she was always careful to make her own decisions. She learned from her mistakes and didn't let setbacks deter her. Whether it was a property deal that didn't go as planned or a mutual fund that underperformed, Shikha always found a way to bounce back, adjust her strategy, and keep moving forward.

A Self-Made Woman: Shikha's Financial Success

By the time Shikha reached her 40s, she had accumulated a significant portfolio. She was no longer just a woman trying to make ends meet after a difficult separation—she was a financially independent, self-made woman with a diverse investment portfolio that included real estate, mutual funds, and traditional savings instruments like FDs.

Shikha's journey wasn't easy, but her determination, discipline, and willingness to learn made all the difference. She didn't come from a background where financial independence was emphasized, but she took control of her financial future and made it a priority. Her ability to adapt, learn from her experiences, and take calculated risks allowed her to build wealth and achieve financial security.

Shikha's success wasn't just about accumulating wealth; it was about gaining control over her life. Her financial independence gave her the freedom to make her own decisions, live life on her own terms, and ensure that she was never again dependent on anyone else for financial support.

Lessons from Shikha Sharma's Journey

Shikha Sharma's life offers several important lessons, especially for women who are looking to achieve financial independence:

1. **Start Small, But Start Early:** Shikha's journey began with small SIP contributions of Rs. 1,000. Over time, as her salary grew, she increased her contributions. The key takeaway here is that it's never too late to start, and even small amounts can grow significantly over time

Neha Agnihotri: The Financially Savvy Investor

Neha Agnihotri's story is one of financial awareness, discipline, and the power of early investing. Born into a financially literate family, Neha was fortunate to have a father who worked as an income tax officer and a banker, making finance a part of her upbringing. Her early exposure to financial concepts like Fixed Deposits, Recurring Deposits, post office savings schemes, and gold investments laid a strong foundation for her future success. Neha's journey from a financially conscious child to a successful professional in the mutual fund industry, and a strong advocate of Systematic Investment Plans (SIPs), offers valuable lessons for women and men alike who seek to achieve financial independence.

This story delves into Neha's upbringing, education, career, and investment strategies, showcasing how her disciplined approach to saving and investing helped her achieve her financial goals and inspire others to follow suit.

Early Life: Financial Awareness from Childhood

Neha Agnihotri's financial journey began long before she earned her first paycheck. Born into a family where finance was part of daily conversations, Neha grew up with a deep understanding of money management. Her father, an income tax officer and a banker, ensured that his children were aware of financial concepts from a young age. Neha's early exposure to financial literacy gave her an edge over many of her peers, who typically began learning about savings and investments only after entering the workforce.

Her father taught her about the importance of saving, and Neha was no stranger to the workings of Fixed Deposits (FDs), Recurring Deposits (RDs), post office saving schemes, and gold investments. From a young age, she knew the value of setting aside a portion of her income for the future. While many children her age were more concerned with spending their allowances, Neha was already thinking about where and how to invest her savings.

This early financial education not only made her aware of the various options available for saving and investing but also instilled in her a mindset that valued long-term financial planning over short-term gratification. She understood that building wealth required patience, discipline, and a diversified approach to managing risk.

Academic Pursuits: MBA in Finance and Marketing

Neha's passion for finance continued into her academic life. She decided to pursue an MBA in finance and marketing from the prestigious Jaipuri Institute of Management in Lucknow. Her education in finance sharpened the knowledge she had acquired as a child and exposed her to more complex financial concepts, including portfolio management, asset allocation, and risk mitigation.

During her MBA program, Neha learned about modern financial tools and how they could be used to create a balanced portfolio. She also developed a strong interest in marketing, which would later serve her well in her professional career. The combination of finance and marketing gave her a holistic understanding of the financial industry, enabling her to navigate both the technical and relational aspects of finance.

Her time at Jaipuri Institute of Management also allowed Neha to network with professors and industry professionals who helped her deepen her understanding of financial markets. This network would play a crucial role later in her career, as it gave her access to mentors and advisors who guided her through the early stages of her professional life.

Early Career: From UTI Bank to Mutual Funds

After completing her MBA, Neha started her career at UTI Bank, where she gained hands-on experience in the banking sector. This was her first professional exposure to the financial services industry, and it gave her a strong foundation in understanding how financial institutions operate. However, Neha's career path took a significant turn when she completed her training at the National Bank for Agriculture and Rural Development (NABARD). This experience broadened her understanding of rural finance and development banking, giving her insights into how finance could be used as a tool for economic development.

Despite her diverse experiences in banking, Neha's true passion lay in investments, particularly in mutual funds. In 2008, she joined SBI Mutual Fund, where she found her calling. This move marked the beginning of her deep dive into the world of mutual funds and investments, and it was here that she began her personal investment journey.

The Beginning of Neha's Investment Journey

Neha's investment journey began early—at just 22 years old. Her first investments were in SBI Magnum Comma Fund and SBI Tax Saver Fund, both of which were introduced to her by a financial advisor. This advisor played a crucial role in shaping Neha's early investment decisions, guiding her on the benefits of diversifying her investments across various asset classes.

In addition to mutual funds, Neha also invested in SBI Life ULIP (Unit Linked Insurance Plan), which offered her both insurance coverage and market-linked returns. She also believed in maintaining a portion of her savings in Fixed Deposits, as they offered security and guaranteed returns. This blend of mutual funds, ULIPs, and FDs provided her with a diversified portfolio that balanced risk and return.

Neha's early investments laid the foundation for her financial future. While many young professionals focus solely on spending their salaries, Neha was focused on building wealth through smart investments. She knew that the earlier she started, the more time her investments would have to grow, thanks to the power of compounding.

The Power of SIPs: A Game-Changer for Neha

Although Neha had already begun investing in mutual funds, her real journey with SIPs (Systematic Investment Plans) started when she joined the mutual fund industry in 2008. As she gained more experience and knowledge about mutual funds, she realized that SIPs were one of the most effective ways to build long-term wealth.

SIPs became her preferred investment tool, and she used them not only for her personal financial goals but also to plan for her family's future. Neha believed in the power of compounding and understood that investing small amounts consistently over time would yield substantial returns. SIPs allowed her to invest in a disciplined manner, and she made it a point to increase her SIP contributions as her income grew.

Neha's approach to SIPs was strategic. She didn't just invest blindly; she carefully selected funds based on her financial goals, risk tolerance, and market conditions. Her SIPs were spread across different types of mutual funds—equity funds for long-term growth, balanced funds for stability, and debt funds for low-risk returns. This diversification ensured that her portfolio was well-balanced and protected against market volatility.

Achieving Family Goals Through SIPs

One of the most significant aspects of Neha's financial planning was how she used SIPs to achieve her family goals. Whether it was saving for her children's education, planning family vacations, or securing her retirement, Neha relied on SIPs to fund these milestones.

For instance, Neha planned and saved for multiple family trips using SIPs. She would start an SIP with a specific goal in mind, such as a family holiday or a large purchase, and contribute regularly. Over time, these SIPs grew, and when the time came, she had the funds she needed without having to dip into her emergency savings or take on debt.

One of the reasons Neha highly recommends SIPs, especially to women, is because they offer a structured way to invest without requiring large lump sums. She often advises her friends and family members to start small and increase their contributions as their financial situation improves. Neha's belief in SIPs is rooted in the idea that investing should be consistent and automatic, making it easier to achieve long-term goals.

Diversification: The Key to Neha's Investment Strategy

Throughout her career, Neha remained a firm believer in the importance of diversifying her investments. She understood that different asset classes—such as equities, debt, real estate, and gold—offered varying levels of risk and return. By spreading her investments across these asset classes, Neha was able to minimize risk while maximizing returns.

Neha's portfolio was a reflection of her risk tolerance and long-term goals. She allocated a portion of her income to high-growth assets like equity mutual funds, while also maintaining a conservative portion in Fixed Deposits and debt funds to provide stability. She invested in ULIPs to ensure that her family had life insurance coverage, while also benefiting from market-linked returns.

One of the key lessons Neha learned was that diversification was not just about spreading money across different types of assets but also about timing and adjusting her portfolio based on market conditions. She regularly reviewed her investments to ensure they were aligned with her goals and made adjustments as needed.

For instance, when the stock market was performing well, Neha increased her exposure to equity funds. Conversely, when markets were volatile, she shifted some of her investments into safer debt funds or FDs to protect her capital. This dynamic approach to diversification allowed her to build a resilient portfolio that could weather market ups and downs.

Neha's Philosophy on Financial Planning for Women

Neha is a strong advocate for women taking control of their financial futures. She believes that financial independence is crucial for women, whether they are working professionals or homemakers. According to Neha, one of the best ways for women to secure their financial future is by making "compulsive investments," meaning regular, automated investments that don't require constant attention.

She encourages women to start with SIPs because they are easy to set up, require minimal initial capital, and allow for gradual growth. Neha often speaks about the importance of starting early, even if the initial investment amount is small. She emphasizes that the key to building wealth is consistency and the power of compounding, which can significantly amplify even small investments over time.

Another key aspect of Neha's philosophy is the importance of financial education. She believes that women should take the time to understand basic financial concepts, such as asset allocation, risk management, and the benefits of diversification. By educating themselves, women can make informed decisions and avoid relying solely on their partners or financial advisors.

Overcoming Challenges and Staying Disciplined

Like any investor, Neha faced challenges along the way. There were times when market volatility tested her resolve, but she remained committed to her long-term goals. One of the key lessons she learned was the importance of staying disciplined during market downturns. Instead of panicking and withdrawing her investments, Neha viewed market corrections as opportunities to invest more at lower prices.

During periods of market downturns, she would often increase her SIP contributions, knowing that buying units at a lower cost would benefit her in the long run when the markets recovered. This disciplined approach helped her avoid emotional decision-making and allowed her to capitalize on market opportunities.

Neha's ability to stay focused on her goals, despite short-term market fluctuations, is one of the reasons she has been able to build a substantial portfolio over the years. She always kept her eyes on the bigger picture, knowing that wealth-building is a marathon, not a sprint.

Neha's Achievements: A Well-Rounded Financial Portfolio

By her mid-30s, Neha had built a well-rounded financial portfolio that included mutual funds, ULIPs, FDs, and real estate. She had achieved many of her financial goals, from funding family vacations to saving for her children's education and securing her retirement.

Her portfolio was diversified across asset classes, ensuring that she was not overly exposed to any one type of investment. Neha's consistent SIP contributions continued to grow, providing her with a steady stream of returns that allowed her to fund both short-term needs and long-term aspirations.

One of her proudest achievements was being able to fund her children's education without taking on any loans. By starting early and investing in SIPs, she was able to accumulate the necessary funds over time, avoiding the stress of last-minute financial planning.

Conclusion: Neha's Legacy of Financial Discipline

Neha Agnihotri's financial journey is a testament to the power of early investing, discipline, and the importance of diversification. From her early days of learning about Fixed Deposits and post office savings schemes to her career in the mutual fund industry, Neha's life has been shaped by a deep understanding of finance and a commitment to long-term wealth-building.

Her story serves as an inspiration to women everywhere, showing that with the right mindset and strategies, financial independence is achievable. Neha's advocacy for SIPs, diversification, and financial education has empowered many women to take control of their finances and secure their futures.

Neha's journey is far from over, but she has already built a strong foundation that will continue to provide for her and her family for years to come. Her story is a reminder that the key to financial success lies not in earning more but in making smart, consistent investments that grow over time.

The Inspiring Journey of Kumkum Chaturvedi: From Theatre Dreams to Financial Success

Kumkum Chaturvedi's life is a compelling story of resilience, self-discovery, and financial wisdom. Born into a middle-class family, she was shaped by her academic prowess and a deep love for the arts, particularly theater. Though her journey took unexpected turns due to family pressures, Kumkum's determination, intelligence, and financial discipline allowed her to build a life of independence and success. This story captures her evolution from a young girl with artistic dreams to a financially savvy woman who found success in teaching, writing, and investing.

Early Life: A Passion for Studies and the Arts

Kumkum was born into a middle-class family, where education was highly valued, and financial stability was often achieved through cautious planning and discipline. From an early age, she demonstrated an exceptional talent for academics. Her parents were proud of her achievements, and Kumkum found joy in excelling at school, but her personality was not limited to being a studious girl. She had another side—a passion for drama, theater, and the performing arts.

Her involvement in theater began during her school years, where she participated in plays and skits, showcasing her talent for acting and her love for the stage. Theater became her escape, a place where she could explore different characters and express herself freely. Kumkum dreamed of making a career in the arts, imagining herself performing on stage and pursuing her passion full-time. She was determined, driven, and ready to take on the world of drama.

However, Kumkum's dreams of pursuing theater as a career soon collided with the realities of family expectations. Coming from a conservative middle-class background, her aspirations were met with resistance. The idea of a career in theater was not seen as a practical or stable choice by her family, who preferred a more conventional path for her future.

Marriage and the End of the Theater Dream

By the time Kumkum reached adulthood, the pressure to settle down and marry became overwhelming. Her family arranged her marriage to a man who held a respectable job with frequent transfers due to his work. Kumkum, though reluctant to leave her passion for theater behind, accepted her family's wishes and got married, marking the end of her journey in the performing arts.

For Kumkum, this marriage was not just the end of her theater aspirations; it also marked a significant change in her personal life. She moved away from her hometown and had to adjust to a new life, a new environment, and the responsibilities that came with marriage. Despite her love for acting and the stage, Kumkum knew she had to prioritize her new life with her husband. The theater dream faded, but her inner drive remained strong.

A New Beginning: Teaching and the Path to Financial Independence

Although she had left theater behind, Kumkum's passion for learning and teaching never wavered. Soon after her marriage, she decided to channel her academic strengths into a career in education. Kumkum began teaching at a local school, where she found fulfillment in helping young minds grow. She was an excellent teacher, known for her dedication and ability to inspire her students.

Teaching also provided Kumkum with financial independence. As soon as she started earning, Kumkum became focused on saving and managing her money. Her parents had always taught her the importance of financial discipline, and she was determined to follow that advice. One of the first steps she took was to invest in Fixed Deposits (FDs) with a bank. She made it a rule to save at least 30% of her monthly income, ensuring that she was building a financial cushion for the future.

Kumkum was careful with her spending, always prioritizing her savings and investments. She viewed her teaching job as not just a source of income but a way to secure her future. Every month, she diligently set aside a portion of her salary for her FDs, allowing her savings to grow steadily over time.

Facing New Challenges: Quitting Teaching Due to Her Husband's Transfers

Kumkum's career in teaching was progressing well, but her husband's job, which required frequent transfers, eventually disrupted her professional life. With each transfer, Kumkum had to quit her teaching position and move to a new city, where finding a new job became increasingly difficult. While she loved teaching, the instability caused by her husband's job meant that her career took a backseat.

Despite this challenge, Kumkum was determined not to let her circumstances hold her back. She was used to adapting and finding new ways to keep herself engaged. She knew that she had to find an alternative way to not only stay productive but also continue her journey toward financial independence.

Reinventing Herself: Becoming a Writer and Earning Royalties

Kumkum's life took another turn when she decided to explore her passion for writing. Having always been good at expressing herself, Kumkum found a new calling in writing educational books for schoolchildren. Drawing on her experience as a teacher, she began writing textbooks for students from class 1 to class 10. Her books were well-received, and soon she was able to secure publishing deals with several educational publishers.

Writing allowed Kumkum to continue contributing to the field of education, even if she was no longer able to teach in the classroom. Her books became popular in schools, and she began earning royalties on the sales of her publications. For Kumkum, writing was more than just a creative outlet—it became a significant source of income that added to her financial stability.

The royalties Kumkum earned from her books provided her with a steady stream of income. True to her disciplined financial habits, she decided to invest this money rather than spend it. She began investing her royalties in mutual funds, recognizing the potential for higher returns compared to traditional savings accounts and FDs.

Transitioning from Fixed Deposits to Mutual Funds

As Kumkum's knowledge of finance grew, so did her understanding of different investment options. While FDs had served her well as a safe and reliable investment, Kumkum realized that they offered limited returns, especially when compared to the potential of mutual funds. She decided to diversify her portfolio and take a more balanced approach to investing.

Kumkum began redeeming her FDs and gradually shifted that money into mutual funds. She knew that mutual funds, though subject to market risks, offered the potential for higher returns over the long term. With the help of financial advisors, Kumkum selected a mix of equity and debt funds to create a diversified portfolio that matched her risk tolerance and financial goals.

Her disciplined approach to investing remained unchanged. Kumkum continued to save and invest a significant portion of her income, ensuring that her portfolio grew steadily over time. She tracked the performance of her mutual funds regularly and adjusted her investments as needed to optimize returns.

Building a Strong Financial Portfolio

Over the years, Kumkum's financial acumen and discipline paid off. Through her writing royalties and strategic investments in mutual funds, she managed to build a substantial financial portfolio. Her diversified approach to investing ensured that her wealth was spread across different asset classes, providing her with both growth and stability.

Kumkum's portfolio included a mix of equity mutual funds for long-term growth, debt funds for stability, and a small portion of fixed-income securities to balance the risk. She continued to reinvest her royalties and savings, allowing her investments to compound over time. By consistently saving and making informed investment decisions, Kumkum was able to achieve financial independence.

One of the key factors behind Kumkum's success was her ability to adapt and evolve. Despite the many challenges she faced, from quitting her teaching job to moving frequently due to her husband's transfers, Kumkum never lost sight of her financial goals. She used each challenge as an opportunity to reinvent herself, whether it was by becoming a writer or by learning more about investing.

A Newfound Freedom: Financial Independence and Personal Fulfillment

Today, Kumkum Chaturvedi is not only financially independent but also creatively fulfilled. Her journey from a young woman with dreams of theater to a successful author and investor is a testament to her resilience and determination. She may have had to leave her passion for acting behind, but she found new ways to express herself and achieve success.

Kumkum's financial independence has given her the freedom to live life on her own terms. She no longer has to worry about financial instability, and her investments provide her with a steady income that allows her to pursue her interests and hobbies. Whether it's writing more books or exploring new creative outlets, Kumkum now has the resources and the confidence to live the life she wants.

Her story is a powerful reminder that even when life doesn't go as planned, it's possible to find new paths to success. Through discipline, adaptability, and a willingness to learn, Kumkum transformed her life from one of limited opportunities to one of financial security and personal fulfillment.

Lessons from Kumkum's Journey

Kumkum Chaturvedi's journey offers valuable lessons for anyone seeking financial independence:

1. **Adaptability is Key:** Kumkum's ability to adapt to changing circumstances allowed her to find new opportunities when her teaching career was interrupted. By reinventing herself as a writer, she created a new source of income that eventually led to financial independence.

2. **The Importance of Saving:** Kumkum's disciplined approach to saving—setting aside 30% of her income each month—was a crucial factor in building her wealth. Her commitment to saving, even when her income was modest, ensured that she always had money to invest.

3. **Diversification Matters:** Kumkum understood the importance of diversifying her investments. By moving from

FDs to mutual funds, she was able to achieve a balance between safety and growth, ensuring that her portfolio was both secure and profitable.

4. **Long-Term Planning Pays Off:** Kumkum's success was not achieved overnight. It was the result of years of consistent saving, smart investing, and careful financial planning. Her story demonstrates the power of patience and long-term thinking when it comes to building wealth.

5. **Long-Term Planning Pays Off:** Kumkum's financial success was the result of disciplined, consistent savings and strategic long-term investments. Her dedication to growing her portfolio through a combination of safe investments like Fixed Deposits and growth-oriented assets like mutual funds allowed her to build significant wealth over time. Her ability to think long-term and delay gratification helped her achieve financial independence. This demonstrates the importance of planning for the future and being patient as your investments grow over time.

6. **Embrace New Opportunities:** Kumkum's decision to move from teaching to writing educational books allowed her to create a new source of income when her teaching career was disrupted. Her openness to learning about investing and exploring new opportunities shows the importance of being adaptable and willing to step out of one's comfort zone to succeed.

7. **Financial Independence is Empowering:** Kumkum's story illustrates how financial independence brings freedom and empowerment. Once Kumkum built her portfolio and secured her financial future, she gained the freedom to

pursue her passions and interests without the pressure of financial instability. She no longer had to depend on others for her financial needs, which gave her the confidence to live life on her own terms.

Conclusion: Kumkum's Legacy of Financial Discipline and Resilience

Kumkum Chaturvedi's story is a powerful example of resilience, financial discipline, and adaptability. Despite facing challenges such as family pressure, the end of her theater dreams, and the need to leave her teaching career, Kumkum remained determined to create a fulfilling life for herself. By embracing new opportunities, saving diligently, and investing wisely, she was able to build a substantial financial portfolio and achieve financial independence.

Her journey shows that setbacks in life can be opportunities in disguise. Even when her theater aspirations were cut short, Kumkum found other ways to express her creativity and achieve success. Her ability to reinvent herself as a teacher, writer, and investor demonstrates the importance of being open to change and taking control of one's financial future.

Kumkum's story also underscores the importance of financial literacy, diversification, and long-term planning. She made informed decisions about her investments, understood the value of spreading risk across different asset classes, and stayed committed to her financial goals. Her disciplined approach to saving and investing serves as an inspiration to anyone looking to secure their financial future.

Today, Kumkum enjoys the fruits of her labor, with a portfolio that provides her with financial stability and the freedom to live life on her own terms. Her story is a reminder that with determination, smart financial choices, and the willingness to adapt, anyone can achieve financial independence and create a life of fulfillment.

A Message to Readers

Kumkum's journey from a young girl with dreams of acting to a financially independent woman is a story of hope and resilience. She overcame challenges, learned from her experiences, and built a successful life for herself. For anyone reading this, know that it is never too late to take control of your financial future. Whether you're starting with small savings or learning about investment options for the first time, the key is to stay disciplined, keep learning, and remain committed to your goals.

Kumkum's story is proof that financial independence is possible for everyone, no matter where you start or what obstacles you face. With the right mindset, determination, and a strategic approach to investing, you too can achieve your dreams and create a future that is both secure and fulfilling.

Kumkum Chaturvedi's life serves as an inspiration for those who seek to achieve financial independence through discipline, smart investments, and a willingness to adapt to changing circumstances. Her story is a testament to the power of resilience and long-term planning in building wealth and securing a brighter future.

Shivani Singh: The Power of Step-Up SIPs and Smart Investing

Shivani Singh's journey from a young girl growing up in a family of bankers to a financially independent woman is an inspiring tale of discipline, early exposure to financial instruments, and a keen interest in the equity markets. Born to parents who both worked in the banking sector, Shivani was introduced to the world of finance from an early age. Her upbringing laid the foundation for a financially savvy life, and her ability to take control of her investments allowed her to create a significant portfolio by the time she reached her mid-twenties.

This story details how Shivani's early interest in banking and investments, particularly her decision to utilize the power of Step-Up SIPs (Systematic Investment Plans), enabled her to build wealth, invest in property, and achieve impressive financial success in a short time.

Early Life: Growing Up in a Financially Literate Family

Shivani was born into a family that lived and breathed finance. With both her mother and father working as bankers, discussions about financial instruments, savings plans, and investment strategies were commonplace in her household. Unlike many children her age, who were more interested in spending their pocket money on toys and treats, Shivani was fascinated by the financial discussions she overheard between her parents. From a young age, she was curious about how money could grow through savings and investments.

Her parents, understanding the importance of financial literacy, made sure that Shivani was introduced to basic banking concepts as she grew older. She was aware of savings accounts, fixed deposits, recurring deposits, and other banking products. However, what caught her interest the most was her father's occasional conversations about the stock market and equity investments. These discussions piqued her curiosity, and by the time she was in class 10th, she knew she wanted to start investing herself.

The First SIP: A Financial Journey Begins

At the age of 15, while still in school, Shivani approached her father with a request. She had been reading about the stock market and mutual funds and wanted to start a Systematic Investment Plan (SIP) of her own. Her father, proud of her initiative, agreed to start a SIP under his guardianship. They began with an amount of Rs. 10,000 per month, a substantial investment for a teenager. This SIP was Shivani's first step into the world of investing, and it set the stage for the financial discipline she would carry throughout her life.

Shivani didn't stop at just starting her SIP. She began educating herself about different types of mutual funds, asset classes, and how the equity market worked. She was eager to learn how SIPs could help her grow wealth over time and was fascinated by the concept of compounding.

The Power of Step-Up SIPs

After completing her graduation, Shivani took up a part-time job to support her expenses and, most importantly, to continue her investments. She knew the importance of consistency in investing and made sure to increase her SIP contribution. Shivani added Rs. 5,000 to her existing Rs. 10,000 SIP, bringing her total monthly investment to Rs. 15,000.

It was during this time that Shivani discovered the concept of a Step-Up SIP. Unlike a regular SIP where the investment amount remains constant, a Step-Up SIP allows the investor to increase the SIP amount by a fixed percentage every year. Shivani immediately saw the potential in this strategy. By increasing her SIP contributions by 20% annually, she could harness the power of compounding to a much greater extent, allowing her portfolio to grow exponentially over time.

She decided to implement this strategy. Every year, without fail, she increased her SIP contributions by 20%, ensuring that her investments kept pace with her growing income. This discipline paid off in ways she hadn't imagined. The Step-Up SIP compounded her wealth at a much faster rate than a regular SIP, and within seven years, her portfolio had earned more than 50% in returns.

Reaping the Rewards: Shivani's First Property Investment

By the time Shivani was in her mid-twenties, her Step-Up SIP strategy had already shown incredible results. Her disciplined investing and the power of compounding had allowed her to build a significant portfolio. With her growing wealth, she decided it was time to take the next step in her financial journey: real estate.

In 2016, Shivani decided to invest in property. She had always dreamed of owning her own home, and now, thanks to her smart investing, she had the means to make that dream a reality. She chose to invest in Dehradun, a city known for its serene environment and rising property values. Using a portion of her portfolio, Shivani booked her first property for Rs. 18 lakhs.

This investment was a major milestone in Shivani's life. Not only was she fulfilling a personal goal, but she was also using the returns from her investments to build an asset that would appreciate over time. The property in Dehradun became an integral part of her portfolio, adding both value and diversity to her investments.

The Big Payoff: Selling the Property for a Huge Return

Shivani's decision to invest in real estate paid off handsomely. Over the next six years, property values in Dehradun soared, and by 2022, the Rs. 18 lakh property she had purchased was now worth Rs. 1 crore. Realizing the incredible return on her investment, Shivani decided to sell the property and book her profits.

This transaction was a turning point for Shivani. The sale of the property not only gave her a substantial financial gain but also reinforced her belief in the power of disciplined investing. By staying committed to her SIPs and making informed investment decisions, she had managed to turn a relatively modest investment into a significant financial windfall.

The proceeds from the property sale allowed Shivani to further diversify her portfolio. She reinvested a portion of the money into mutual funds, ensuring that her wealth continued to grow. She also began exploring other investment avenues, such as equity investments and real estate, to ensure her portfolio remained balanced and robust.

The Importance of Financial Discipline

Shivani's success story is a testament to the power of financial discipline and the importance of starting early. From her first SIP at the age of 15 to her decision to implement a Step-Up SIP strategy, Shivani's journey demonstrates that consistent, disciplined investing can lead to significant financial growth over time.

Her approach to investing wasn't about taking shortcuts or trying to time the market. Instead, Shivani focused on the long-term, making regular contributions to her SIPs and allowing compounding to do its work. This disciplined approach, combined with her decision to increase her SIP contributions by 20% each year, allowed her to maximize the growth potential of her investments.

Empowering Women Through Financial Literacy

Shivani's story is not just about personal success—it's also about empowerment. Throughout her journey, Shivani has been a strong advocate for financial literacy, particularly for women. She believes that every woman should understand the power of investing and the benefits of SIPs as a tool for building long-term wealth.

Shivani often speaks about the importance of women taking control of their finances and making informed decisions about their money. She encourages women to start investing early, even if the initial amounts are small. According to Shivani, the key is consistency—making regular investments and increasing contributions over time.

Her message to women is clear: "Don't wait for the perfect time to start investing. Start now, start small, and watch your money grow."

Lessons from Shivani's Journey

Shivani Singh's journey offers valuable lessons for anyone looking to achieve financial success:

1. **Start Early**: Shivani's financial journey began when she was just 15 years old. Starting early allowed her to take full advantage of the power of compounding, which played a significant role in growing her wealth over time.

2. **Step-Up SIPs Are Powerful**: By increasing her SIP contributions by 20% each year, Shivani was able to accelerate the growth of her portfolio. This strategy allowed her to compound her wealth at a much faster rate than a regular SIP.

3. **Discipline is Key**: Shivani's success was built on consistent, disciplined investing. She made regular contributions to her SIPs, even during periods of market volatility, and this discipline paid off in the long run.

4. **Diversify Your Portfolio**: Shivani didn't rely solely on mutual funds. She diversified her portfolio by investing in real estate, which allowed her to benefit from the appreciation of property values in addition to her SIP returns.

5. **Financial Independence is Empowering**: Shivani's journey shows that taking control of your finances can lead to incredible opportunities. Her disciplined investing allowed her to achieve financial independence and make life-changing decisions, such as buying and selling property.

Conclusion: Shivani's Ongoing Financial Journey

Today, Shivani Singh continues to build her financial portfolio, always exploring new investment opportunities and staying true to the principles of disciplined investing. Her journey is far from over, but her early success has set her on a path toward financial freedom and long-term wealth.

Shivani's story is a powerful reminder that financial success is within reach for anyone who is willing to start early, stay disciplined, and make informed decisions. Whether you're just starting your investment journey or looking to take your portfolio to the next level, Shivani's experience demonstrates the power of SIPs and the importance of being proactive with your money.

Through her journey, Shivani has not only secured her own financial future but has also become a role model for other women who aspire to achieve financial independence. Her story is proof that with the right mindset and approach, anyone can build wealth and create a secure, prosperous future.

www.ingramcontent.com/pod-product-compliance
Lightning Source LLC
LaVergne TN
LVHW061345080526
838199LV00094B/7370